"For the mama who whispers 'I'm so tired'..."

You're not a Bad Mom You're Just Tired

A Compassionate Guide to Healing Burnout and Finding Yourself Again

You're not a Bad Mom, Youre just Tired

A Compassionate Guide to
Healing Burnout
and Finding Yourself Again

Written by Zandra Mae Cochrane

All rights reserved. No part of this book may be reproduced, stored in a retrieval system,
or transmitted in any form or by any means—electronic, mechanical, photocopying, recording, or otherwise—without prior written permission of the publisher.

ISBN: 978-1-7645195-0-2
Printed in Australia
First edition, 2025

For every mother who has ever cried in silence, doubted herself, or felt invisible. You were never failing — you were just tired.
This book is for you.

For every mother who has ever whispered,
"I'm so tired."
This book is your permission to rest, to breathe,
and to come back to yourself.
You are not alone.
You are not failing.
You are loved

Motherhood changed me in ways I never expected. It stretched me, softened me, broke me open, and rebuilt me again. Same as you, it also exhausted me — not just physically, but emotionally, mentally, and spiritually. Nobody told me all the plot twist that I have expected as a mother.

There were days I felt like I was disappearing inside the role of "mom," days when I wondered if I was doing enough, and days when I questioned if I was even good at this. Imagine the 24/7 role we had to do not just at home but in the lives of our family.

I'm a mother of two — a teenage boy and a young girl — and at the time of writing this, I'm also pregnant with my third. My eldest is sixteen, navigating independence, identity, and all the complexities of becoming a young woman. My second is six, full of energy, questions, and the kind of clinginess that only a young child can give. And in between their two worlds, I often find myself pulled in opposite directions.

Some days, I feel like I'm switching between two different versions of motherhood — the one who needs to be calm and wise for a teenager, and the one who needs to be playful and patient for a little boy.

And then there's the version of me who is pregnant, hormonal, tired, and just trying to survive the day. There are mornings when I can't even finish my coffee or meal just to run things. I'm sure some of you here have felt this way, some may be running so much with tasks such as sending kids to school, packing their lunchboxes, or pumping like a milk machine because you're breastfeeding with a little one. I felt like more than a housemaid than a mother...

There are afternoons when I realize I haven't brushed my hair. There are nights when I collapse into bed wondering if I did enough, gave enough, or was enough. And maybe you've felt that too.

I wrote this not as an expert mother looking down, but as a mother standing beside you. I've lived the guilt, the overwhelm, the pressure to be everything, the cultural expectations, and the quiet fear that maybe I wasn't doing motherhood "right."

But here's the truth I learned: You're not a bad mom. You're just tired. And tired mothers don't need judgment — they need compassion, understanding, and a safe place to breathe.

Introduction

There's a moment in every mother's life when she looks around her home — the toys on the floor, the dishes in the sink, the laundry waiting to be folded — and feels a heaviness settle in her chest. Not because she doesn't love her family, but because she's tired in a way that sleep alone can't fix.

I know that moment well.

Before I became pregnant again, I was a full-time working mama juggling deadlines, responsibilities, and the emotional weight of raising two kids — a teenager and a young child. And in between those two worlds, I often felt like I was being stretched thin.

There were days I'd come home from work, drop my bag by the door, and just stand there — staring at the mess, the chaos, the unfinished tasks — wondering, "When will everything ever be finished?"

Again, I'd like you to remember this:
You're not a bad mom. You're just tired.

Tired from doing your best. Tired from loving deeply. Tired from holding everything together. Tired from functioning like a robot. Tired from being the anchor for everyone else.

This book is not here to judge you or tell you to "do better."

It's here to help you understand why you feel this way, to give language to the exhaustion you've been carrying, and to guide you gently back to yourself.

Because you also deserve rest.
You deserve compassion.
You deserve to feel like you again.

And I hope that as you read these pages, you'll finally see what I had to learn the hard way:

You were never failing.
You were simply exhausted — and you deserve to heal.

Chapter 1
The Mental Load No One Sees

There's a kind of tired that doesn't show up in photos. It doesn't look like messy hair or dark circles in your eyes or unfinished chores. It's the tired that lives inside your mind — the kind that comes from carrying everything, remembering everything, planning everything, and holding everything together even when you feel like falling apart.

This is the mental load.
And if you're a mother, you know it well.

As mothers, we all have that Invisible Checklist, and that is the mental load running in your head from the moment you wake up to the moment you finally collapse into bed.

Im sure you are all familiar with this sounds:
- Did I sign the school form?
- What will they eat for dinner?
- Did I reply to that message?
- When is the next doctor's appointment?
- Is the uniform washed?
- Did I forget something?
- What else do I need to do?

And it never stops. Even when you sit down, your mind doesn't. Even when you rest, your brain is still working. Even when you're quiet, you're thinking for everyone else.

That's the part no one sees.

That's the part that makes you tired even when you haven't moved.

Modern Motherhood Is Mentally Heavy

Motherhood today is not all the same as it was for our parents or grandparents.

Modern moms are expected to:
- Work like they don't have kids ; Parent like they don't have a job; Keep the house clean; Stay emotionally available; Be patient, gentle, and present
- Manage school schedules
- Handle digital safety
- Cook healthy meals
- Maintain relationships
- Look put-together

And somehow still "take care of themselves". It's too much. It's more than any one person can carry — yet mothers carry it anyway.

Whever I whisper to myself, "When will everything ever be finished?"
A part of me is saying "But motherhood doesn't have a finish line." There is always something waiting. Something to clean. Something to fix. Something to remember. Something to worry about.

And that's why you're tired — not because you're weak, but because you're carrying more than anyone realizes.

You're Not Imagining It — It Really Is Heavy

The mental load is real. It's invisible, but it's heavy. It's silent, but it's exhausting. It's unseen, but it affects everything — your mood, your energy, your patience, your confidence, your sense of self. And the hardest part? Most mothers carry it alone. Not because they want to, but because they feel they have to. Because they believe no one else will do it right. Because they don't want to burden anyone. Because they think it's "just part of being a mom."

But mama...
You were never meant to carry all of this by yourself.

You're not tired because you're doing nothing. You're tired because you're doing everything — even the things no one sees. You're not failing. You're not lazy. You're not unorganized. You're not dramatic.

You're carrying the mental load of an entire household. And that is real work.

This chapter is your permission to acknowledge it. To name it. To stop minimizing it. To stop pretending you're okay when you're drowning inside. Because healing begins with honesty.

And the truth is:
You're tired because you're carrying too much — not because you're not enough.

Reflection

Take a moment to breathe and answer these gently:

1. What are the top five things you mentally carry every day that no one sees?
2. Which part of your mental load feels the heaviest right now?
3. What would it feel like to share even one of these responsibilities with someone else?

A Short Prayer for the Tired Mind

"Lord, You see the weight I carry even when no one else does.
Give me strength for the things I must do,
wisdom for the things I can let go,
and courage to ask for help when I need it.
Quiet my mind, calm my heart,
and remind me that I don't have to carry everything alone."

Mama Reminder

Your mind is tired because it works so hard for everyone you love.
Give yourself grace — you're doing more than enough.

Chapter 2
The Guilt Olympics Cycle

Welcome to The Guilt Olympics — where moms win gold every day without even trying.

You know the drill:
- You give your kid nuggets or unhealthy food for dinner → Guilt.
- You hide in the bathroom for 3 minutes → Guilt.
- You say "Not now, mama's tired" → Guilt.
- You breathe wrong → Guilt.

Meanwhile, your kids are fine.

They're fed, alive, and probably watching Bluey for the 47th time. But YOU? You're over here feeling like you've failed motherhood because you didn't cut their sandwich into a heart shape.

Mama...
Relax.
You're doing amazing.

And if guilt tries to talk to you today, tell it:
"Not now. I'm busy keeping tiny humans alive."

There's a moment in motherhood when guilt becomes so normal, you don't even notice it anymore. It slips into your thoughts while you're washing dishes, while you're scrolling your phone, while you're lying in bed trying to fall asleep.

It sounds like: "I should have been more patient." "I shouldn't have raised my voice." "I should be spending more time with them." "I should be doing better."

Modern motherhood has turned guilt into a daily companion — one that sits beside you, whispers in your ear, and convinces you that you're always falling short.

Where Does This Guilt Come From?
Guilt comes from everywhere:

a. Social Media
You see moms baking organic muffins, doing Montessori activities, and smiling in spotless living rooms.
Meanwhile, you're reheating leftovers and stepping on different toys on the floor.

b. Cultural Expectations
Filipina moms like me or asian moms are raised to be strong, selfless, and endlessly patient. We're taught to "tiisin mo na lang," which means "Just take it" even when we're drowning.

3. Internal Pressure

You want to be the best mom you can be — and that desire becomes a weight.

4. Comparison

You compare your worst moments to someone else's highlight reel. And slowly, guilt becomes your default emotion.

The Lie Guilt Tells You

Guilt tells you: "You're not doing enough. But the truth is: You're doing more than anyone sees. More than anyone acknowledges. More than you give yourself credit for.

Guilt makes you forget that motherhood is not a performance — it's a relationship. And relationships are messy, imperfect, and human.

The Day I Realized Guilt Was Controlling Me

One afternoon, after a long day of work from teaching, I came home exhausted. My teenager was moody already. My six-year-old wanted attention. He has mild auytism. The house was a mess.

Now, I am pregnant, hormonal, and overwhelmed. I snapped. Not loudly. Not dramatically. Just a tired, frustrated sigh. And instantly — guilt. "You should have handled that better." "You're the adult." "You're the mom."

But then I paused.

I realized I wasn't guilty because I did something wrong. I was guilty because I expected myself to be superhuman. And mama...
You are not meant to be superhuman.
You are meant to be real.

Let us break that Guilt Cycle. Here's the truth:
- You will get tired.
- You will get overwhelmed.
- You will lose your patience.
- You will make mistakes.

And none of that makes you a bad mom.
It makes you a human mom — the only kind that exists.
The guilt cycle breaks when you replace guilt with grace.
Human Grace says:
"I'm still learning."
"I'm still trying."
"I'm still growing."
"I'm allowed to be imperfect."
And that shift changes everything.

Reflection

Take a moment to breathe and answer these gently:

1. Where is guilt stealing your peace today?

A Short Prayer for the Tired Mind

"Lord, lift the weight of guilt from my heart.
Help me see myself the way You see me — loved, forgiven, and growing.
Teach me to give myself grace in the moments I fall short."

Mama Reminder

GRACE IS STRONGER THAN GUILT.
LET IT HOLD YOU TODAY.

Chapter 3
Cultural Expectations That Exhaust Us

"Just deal with it!" is not a personality trait — it's a wound we inherited.

There's a unique kind of exhaustion that mothers carry — one that doesn't come from sleepless nights or endless chores, but from the weight of expectations passed down through generations.

If you grew up in a Filipino household, you know exactly what I mean.

We were raised to be strong.
We were raised to be selfless.
We were raised to endure.
We were raised to put everyone else first.
We were raised to smile even when we were breaking inside.

And somewhere along the way, we learned that motherhood meant carrying everything without complaint.

The "Ilaw ng Tahanan" Pressure

Filipina moms are often called the ilaw ng tahanan — the light of the home.

It sounds beautiful, but it also carries a silent message:
You must always be bright.
You must always be warm.
You must always be available.
You must always be okay.

But mama... even lights burn out when they're never switched off.

The Culture of Endurance

Growing up, we heard it everywhere:
"Just deal with it."
"Mom is always like that."
"That's just normal."
"You can do it."

These phrases were meant to encourage us, but they also taught us to:

Ignore our needs
Silence our pain
Hide our exhaustion
Accept unfair burdens
Pretend we're okay even when we're not

Modern motherhood is already heavy — but when you add cultural expectations, the weight becomes overwhelming

The Silent Rules We Inherited

Without realizing it, many of us follow these unspoken rules:
- A good mom sacrifices everything
- A good mom doesn't complain
- A good mom is always patient
- A good mom keeps the house perfect
- A good mom never asks for help
- A good mom puts herself last

But these rules were created in a different time — a time when mothers didn't have to juggle full-time jobs, digital parenting, emotional labor, and the pressure to be "present" 24/7.

Modern motherhood is different.
Modern moms are carrying more than ever.
And yet, the expectations stayed the same.

As a working mother of two — with a teenager and a young child — and now pregnant again, I've felt this pressure deeply. There were days I'd come home from work exhausted, only to hear that little voice in my head say:
"You should still cook." "You should clean." "You should be patient."

"You should be grateful."
"You should do more."

But where did these "shoulds" come from? Not from my heart. Not from my children. Not from God. They came from expectations I inherited — expectations that were never meant to define my worth.

You Are Allowed to Break the Cycle

You are allowed to rest.
You are allowed to ask for help.
You are allowed to say "I'm tired."
You are allowed to set boundaries.
You are allowed to be human.

Breaking cultural expectations doesn't mean you're rejecting your roots. It means you're healing them. It means you're choosing a healthier, kinder version of motherhood — one that doesn't require you to disappear in the process.

You don't have to be the perfect mom. You don't have to carry everything alone. You don't have to endure silently. You don't have to meet impossible standards. You are allowed to redefine motherhood in a way that honors your wellbeing, not just your responsibilities. You are allowed to be the light of your home — without burning yourself out.

Reflection

Take a moment to breathe and answer these gently:

1. What cultural expectations did you grow up with about motherhood?
2. Which of these expectations feel heavy or unrealistic today?
3. What would motherhood look like if you allowed yourself more grace?

A Short Prayer for the Mama carrying cultural pressure

"Lord, help me release the expectations that exhaust me.
Give me courage to break unhealthy patterns
and wisdom to create new ones rooted in love, not pressure.
Teach me that I am enough — even when I am tired, imperfect, and still learning."

Mama Reminder

You don't have to live up to a version of motherhood that hurts you.
You are allowed to choose a gentler way.

Chapter 4
The Identity you lost without noticing

Motherhood didn't erase you — it just buried you under everything you've been carrying.

There's a quiet moment in motherhood when you suddenly realize you don't recognize yourself anymore.

Not because you've changed physically — though that happens too — but because somewhere between the sleepless nights, the school runs, the tantrums, the teenage moods, the deadlines, the chores, and the constant giving...
> you disappeared.

> Not all at once.
> Not dramatically.
> Just slowly, quietly, piece by piece.

The Slow Disappearance of "You" starts with small things:
> You stop doing your hobbies.
> You stop buying things for yourself.
> You stop resting.
> You stop saying what you need.
> You stop prioritizing your dreams.

Then it becomes bigger:
You stop recognizing your emotions.
You stop feeling connected to your body.
You stop remembering what you used to enjoy.
You stop feeling like the woman you once were.

And one day, you look in the mirror and think:
"Where did I go?"

Modern Motherhood Makes It Easy to Lose Yourself

Mothers today are expected to be:
The emotional anchor
The household manager
The scheduler
The cook
The cleaner
The comforter
The teacher
The therapist
The nurse
The everything . . .

And if you're a working mom — like you were before this pregnancy — the pressure doubles.
You wake up early, rush through the day, come home exhausted, and still feel like you have to give more.

You stand in the middle of a messy house after work, staring at everything that needs to be done, wondering:

"When will I ever get a break?"

And in that constant cycle of doing, doing, doing...you forget how to simply be.

As a mother of two — a teenager and a young child — and now pregnant again, I've lived this deeply.

There were days before I'd come home from work and feel like I was switching between three different versions of myself:
- The calm, wise mother for my teenager
- The playful, patient mother for my six-year-old
- The tired, hormonal, overwhelmed mother growing another life

And somewhere in between those roles, I realized I didn't know who I was anymore.

I wasn't the woman I used to be.
I wasn't the woman I wanted to be.
I was just... surviving.

And maybe you've felt that too.

Losing Yourself Doesn't Mean You Failed

It means you've been giving so much of yourself to everyone else that there was nothing left for you.

It means you've been loving deeply. It means you've been trying your best. It means you've been carrying more than anyone sees.

Motherhood didn't erase you —
it just buried you under responsibilities that were never meant to be carried alone.

The Grief No One Talks About

There's a kind of grief in motherhood that feels strange to admit:

- Grieving your old freedom
- Grieving your old body
- Grieving your old dreams
- Grieving the version of you who had time, energy, and space

This grief doesn't mean you don't love your children. It means you miss yourself — and that is allowed.

Finding Yourself Again Starts With Permission

Permission to rest.
Permission to say no.
Permission to ask for help.
Permission to take up space.
Permission to have dreams outside motherhood.
Permission to be more than "mama."

You don't have to choose between being a good mother and being a whole woman. You can be both — but only if you stop abandoning yourself.

> You are still in there.
> Under the exhaustion.
> Under the responsibilities.
> Under the expectations.
> Under the guilt.
> Under the pressure.
> The woman you were —
> the woman you are —
> is waiting to be seen again.
>
> And she deserves to come back.

Reflection

Take a moment to breathe and answer these gently:

1. What parts of yourself have you lost or forgotten since becoming a mother?
2. What did you love doing before motherhood that you haven't done in years?
3. What would it look like to give yourself even 10 minutes a day to reconnect with yourself?

A Short Prayer for the Mama who feels lost

"Lord, help me find the parts of myself I've forgotten.
Show me who I am beyond my responsibilities.
Give me courage to care for myself and wisdom to honor the woman inside the mother.
Guide me back to myself with gentleness and grace."

Mama Reminder

You didn't lose yourself on purpose —
you were just busy loving everyone else.
Now it's time to love yourself, too.

Chapter 5
The Mindset traps that drain you daily

Sometimes the loudest pressure doesn't come from the world — it comes from inside your own mind.

There's a kind of exhaustion that doesn't come from chores, schedules, or physical work. It comes from the thoughts you carry. The expectations you place on yourself. The silent standards you try to meet every single day.

Modern motherhood is not just physically demanding — it's mentally demanding. And the hardest part is that so much of the pressure comes from within.

These are the mindset traps that drain mothers without them even realizing it.

a. The Perfectionism Trap – "I should be doing better." Perfectionism always whispers:
"The house should be clean."
"I should be more patient."
"I should be more organized."
"I should be doing more activities with the kids."
"I should be handling everything gracefully."

But perfectionism is a thief. It steals your joy. It steals your peace. It steals your ability to see how much you're already doing.

You don't need to be perfect.
You just need to be present — and even that doesn't have to be 24/7.

b. The Comparison Trap – "Other moms seem to be doing it better."

Comparison is everywhere — especially online. You see: Moms with spotless homes; Moms doing Pinterest-worthy activities; Moms who look put-together; Moms who seem endlessly patient; Moms who "bounce back" after pregnancy

And suddenly, your real life feels inadequate.
But here's the truth:
- You're comparing your behind-the-scenes to someone else's highlight reel.

You don't see their tears.
You don't see their exhaustion.
You don't see their struggles.
You only see the curated moments.

And your real, messy, beautiful motherhood is not less valuable.

c. The Over-Functioning Trap – "If I don't do it, no one will."

This trap convinces you that, You must handle everything, You must be the responsible one, You must be the strong one, You must be the one who remembers everything, You must be the one who fixes everything.

And before you know it, you're doing the work of three people — silently, automatically, without question.

Over-functioning is not strength.
It's survival mode.
And you deserve more than survival.

d. The People-Pleasing Trap – "I don't want to disappoint anyone."

Mothers often feel responsible for everyone's emotions:
- You don't want your kids upset
- You don't want your partner stressed
- You don't want your family judging you
- You don't want to be seen as "lazy" or "uncaring"

So you say yes when you're tired. You give when you're empty. You stretch yourself thin to keep everyone else comfortable.

But mama...
Your comfort matters too.

e. The "Strong Mom" Trap – "I should be able to handle this."

This is the mindset we inherit from culture: "Just deal with it. ""You can do it.""That's a m other should be."

Now slowly, we don't realised that , Strength becomes a mask. A shield. A prison. You push through even when you're breaking. You endure even when you're exhausted. You stay silent even when you need help.

But strength doesn't mean suffering quietly. Strength means knowing when to rest.

Believed it or not, as a working mom of two — with a teenager and a young child — and now pregnant again, I've fallen into every one of these traps.

There were days before I'd come home from work and think: "I should still clean"; "I should still cook."; "I should be more patient."; "I should be doing more." And when I couldn't, I felt guilty. I felt inadequate. I felt like I was failing.

But honestly, I realised I wasn't failing — I was just exhausted from fighting battles inside my own mind. And maybe you've been fighting them too.

Now, let us all break free from those Mindset traps

Freedom begins with awareness. You can't change what you don't see. You can't heal what you don't name. You can't rest if you believe you're not allowed to.

This chapter is your invitation to:
"Release perfection"
"Stop comparing"
"Share the load"
"Honor your needs"
"Redefine strength"

You don't have to be everything. You don't have to do everything. You don't have to carry everything. You are allowed to be human.

Reflection

Take a moment to breathe and answer these gently:

1. Which mindset trap do you fall into most often?
2. How does it affect your daily life and energy?
3. What would change if you gave yourself permission to let go of that expectation?

A Short Prayer for the Mama fighting silent battles

"Lord, help me recognize the thoughts that exhaust me.
Give me wisdom to release the expectations that are not mine to carry.
Teach me to be gentle with myself and to see myself through Your eyes —
capable, loved, and enough."

Mama Reminder

You don't have to be perfect to be a good mom.
You just have to be you —
tired, trying, learning, growing, and loving.

Chapter 6
The Emotional Labor of Loving Everyone

You carry everyone's feelings — but who carries yours?

There's a kind of exhaustion that doesn't come from cleaning, cooking, or working. It comes from feeling. Feeling everything. For everyone. All the time.

This is emotional labor — the invisible work mothers do that no one talks about, but every mother feels. It's the weight of:
- Managing everyone's moods
- Anticipating everyone's needs
- Keeping the peace
- Absorbing stress
- Being the emotional anchor
- Staying calm even when you're overwhelmed
- Being strong even when you're breaking

And mind you, it is exhausting . . . .

In many families — especially Filipino families — the mother is the emotional center. You're the one who: notices when someone is upset, softens your tone to avoid conflict, mediates arguments, comforts hurt feelings, encourages, reassures, uplifts and keeps the family emotionally connected. You're the one who holds the home together — not just physically, but emotionally. But being the emotional anchor means you absorb a lot of weight. And anchors get heavy.

A lot of us have seen this "Invisible Work" that no one sees. That is sometimes also calles as Emotional labor which looks like:
- Staying patient when your teenager slams the door
- Staying gentle when your six-year-old cries for the third time today
- Staying calm when your partner is stressed
- Staying composed when everything feels chaotic
- Staying strong when you want to fall apart

It's the work of holding everyone else's emotions while suppressing your own. It's the work of being the safe place for everyone — even when you don't feel safe inside yourself.

In my own experience, sometimes I've felt emotional labor in every season. There were days before when my teenager was moody and distant; my six-year-old needed constant attention; my partner was stressed from work; my body was tired from hormonal changes and my mind was overwhelmed from everything I was carrying.

And yet, I still felt responsible for keeping the peace.

I still felt responsible for staying calm. I still felt responsible for making sure everyone else was okay. But who was making sure I was okay? That's the question emotional labor forces us to confront. And this is why Emotional Labor Drains You:

- Because it's constant.
- Because it's invisible.
- Because it's unacknowledged.
- Because it's expected.
- Because it's heavy.
- Because it's lonely.

And because mothers are often taught that their emotions should come last. But your emotions matter. Your feelings matter. Your heart matters.

Remember, You cannot pour from an empty cup —
and emotional labor empties the cup faster than anything else

You Are Allowed to Feel Too

You don't have to be the calm one all the time. You don't have to be the strong one every day. You don't have to be the emotional sponge for everyone else's stress. You don't have to hold everything together alone. You are allowed to Cry, Break down, Ask for help, Say "I'm overwhelmed", Take a short break and Feel your feelings.

You are not a robot.
You are a human mother with a human heart.
And your heart deserves care too.

This passage wants you to know that:
"You are not tired because you're weak."
"You are tired because you've been carrying the emotional weight of an entire family."
"You are not failing."
"You are not dramatic."
"You are not "too sensitive."
"You are emotionally overloaded —
and that is a real, valid, human experience."
"You deserve support."
"You deserve rest."
"You deserve to be cared for too…"

Reflection

TAKE A MOMENT TO BREATHE AND ANSWER THESE GENTLY:

1. WHOSE EMOTIONS DO YOU CARRY BESIDES YOUR OWN?
2. WHAT FEELINGS HAVE YOU BEEN SUPPRESSING TO KEEP THE PEACE?
3. WHAT WOULD IT LOOK LIKE TO LET SOMEONE ELSE SUPPORT YOU EMOTIONALLY?

A Short Prayer for the Mama carrying everyone's feelings

"Lord, You see the emotions I carry — the ones I speak and the ones I hide.
Give me strength to release what is not mine,
courage to feel what I've been holding back,
and comfort for the parts of me that are tired from loving so deeply.
Teach me that I am worthy of emotional rest too."

Mama Reminder

You don't have to hold everyone together.
You deserve someone who holds you too.

Chapter 7
What your body has been trying to tell you

Your body whispers long before it ever screams.

There comes a point in motherhood when your body starts sending signals you can't ignore anymore. Not because you're weak. Not because you're failing. But because you've been carrying more than any one person was ever meant to carry.

And your body — loyal, loving, and patient — has been trying to tell you. Sometimes softly. Sometimes urgently. Sometimes in ways you don't understand until you finally pause long enough to listen.

Your Body Has a Language of Its Own

Motherhood is not just emotional work. It's not just mental work. It's not just physical work. It's all of it at once. And your body keeps track of every part:

- Every sleepless night
- Every rushed morning
- Every tantrum you soothed
- Every teenage mood you navigated
- Every meal you prepared

- Every worry you carried
- Every responsibility you held
- Every moment you put yourself last

Your body remembers. Even when you try to push through. Even when you tell yourself "I'm fine." Even when you ignore the signs. Your body doesn't forget.

The Subtle Signs You've Been Ignoring

Your body speaks in whispers first:
- A tightness in your chest
- A heaviness in your shoulders
- A fog in your mind
- A shortness of breath
- A sudden wave of overwhelm
- A headache that lingers
- A back that aches
- A heart that races
- A fatigue that sleep doesn't fix

These are not random. These are not "just part of being a mom." These are messages. Your body is saying: "I'm tired." "I'm overloaded." "I need rest." "I need care too.

Modern Motherhood Overloads the Nervous System

Mothers today live in constant stimulation:
- Noise
- Clutter
- Notifications from either phone or social medias
- Questions
- Emotional demands
- Mental reminders
- Multitasking
- Pressure to be "on" all the time

Your nervous system never gets a break. This is why, because small things feel big, you snap faster, you cry easily, you feel overwhelmed by noise, you crave silence, you feel drained even after sleeping and your body isn't malfunctioning. It's protecting you.

It's saying:
"You've been in survival mode too long."

Sometimes, I've felt this deeply before. There were days when:
- My back felt like it was carrying the world
- My chest felt tight for no reason
- My patience was thin even when I tried my best
- My senses felt overloaded by simple noise
- My body felt heavy even after resting

And I would think: "Why am I like this?" "Why can't I handle things better?" "What's wrong with me?" But nothing was wrong. My body was simply speaking — loudly — after years of being ignored. And maybe your body has been speaking too.

Your Body Is Not the Enemy — It's Your Messenger

Your body is not betraying you. Your body is not weak. Your body is not failing. Your body is communicating. It's saying:

"Slow down."
"Breathe."
"Let go of what's too heavy."
"Ask for help."
"Rest without guilt."
"Take care of me the way you take care of everyone else."

Your body is your partner in motherhood — not your burden.

Listening to Your Body Is an Act of Love

You don't have to wait until you break down. You don't have to wait until you're sick. You don't have to wait until you're overwhelmed. You can listen now. Listening to your body is not selfish. It's not indulgent. It's not weakness. It's wisdom. It's strength. It's survival.

*Because when you care for your body,
you care for the mother your children depend on.*

Reflection

TAKE A MOMENT TO BREATHE AND ANSWER THESE GENTLY:

1. WHAT PHYSICAL SIGNS HAS YOUR BODY BEEN SHOWING YOU LATELY?
2. WHAT EMOTIONS MIGHT BE HIDING BEHIND THOSE PHYSICAL SENSATIONS?
3. WHAT IS ONE SMALL WAY YOU CAN HONOR YOUR BODY THIS WEEK?

A Short Prayer for the Mama whose body is tired

"LORD, THANK YOU FOR THIS BODY THAT CARRIES ME THROUGH MOTHERHOOD.
HELP ME HEAR ITS WHISPERS BEFORE THEY BECOME CRIES.
GIVE ME COURAGE TO REST,
WISDOM TO SLOW DOWN,
AND COMPASSION FOR THE PARTS OF ME THAT FEEL WORN OUT.
TEACH ME TO CARE FOR MYSELF WITH THE SAME TENDERNESS I GIVE MY CHILDREN."

Mama Reminder

Your body is tired because it has been loving, giving, and carrying so much. Treat it with the same gentleness you offer everyone else.

Chapter 8
The Mental Load You Carry Without Realizing it

Your mind is doing more work than anyone sees.

There's a kind of exhaustion that doesn't show up in the laundry basket or the sink full of dishes. It doesn't make noise. It doesn't leave a mess. It doesn't announce itself. It lives quietly inside your mind.

This is the mental load — the invisible, constant, never-ending list of responsibilities that mothers carry every single day. It's the planning. The remembering. The anticipating. The organizing. The worrying. The checking. The preparing. The thinking for everyone. And it is heavy

The Mental Load Is the Work No One Sees

The mental load is not the task itself — it's the thinking behind the task. It's not just making dinner, doing laundry, getting kids ready and managing schedules. But, it's:

- "What ingredients do we have?"
- "What time does the laundry need to finish so uniforms dry

- "Does she have her library bag today?"
- "Did I sign that permission slip?"
- "Is there enough bread for tomorrow?"
- "What time is the appointment again?"
- "Did I reply to that message?"
- "Who needs what from me next?"

Your brain is constantly running in the background — like a computer with too many tabs open. And eventually, it overheats.

And why mothers carry the mental load?

>Because you're the one who notices.
>Because you're the one who remembers.
>Because you're the one who anticipates.
>Because you're the one who cares.

And often, because you're the one who has always done it. In many families — especially Filipino families — the mother is the default: Default planner, Default organizer, Default scheduler, Default problem-solver, Default emotional support and Default everything

Not because others don't love you, but because you've been the one holding it all together for so long.

The Mental Load Is Why You're Tired Even When You "Did Nothing"

Have you ever had a day where you didn't do much physically, but still felt exhausted? That's the mental load. It drains you even when your body is still. Because your mind is never still. You're always: Thinking ahead, Preventing problems, Managing emotions, Keeping track of details, Holding everyone's needs in your head

Your brain is doing the work of five people — quietly, constantly, without applause. No wonder you're tired.

There were days before when I would sit down after work and think: "Why am I so tired? I barely did anything today."
But then I'd remember:
- I planned meals in my head
- I remembered school events
- I checked my calendar three times
- I worried about my teenager's mood
- I mentally prepared for bedtime routines
- I kept track of appointments
- I reminded myself to buy groceries
- I carried everyone's needs in my mind

And suddenly, the exhaustion made sense. My mind had been working nonstop — even when my body wasn't. Maybe your mind has been doing the same

Let me remind you that the mental load is not your fault. You didn't choose it. You didn't ask for it. You didn't create it alone.

It's the result ofnCultural expectations, Family patterns, Gender roles, Motherhood norms, Emotional responsibility, Habit and Love.

You carry the mental load because you care.
But caring shouldn't mean carrying everything alone

Please mama, you are 100% allowed to share the load. Sharing the mental load doesn't mean you're weak. It doesn't mean you're failing. It doesn't mean you're less of a mother. It means you're human.

You are allowed to:
- Delegate
- Ask for help
- Say "I can't hold all of this"
- Let others take responsibility
- Release the pressure to remember everything

You don't have to be the family's walking calendar
You don't have to be the default brain.
You don't have to carry the invisible weight alone

This Chapter Wants You to Know that your mind is tired because it has been working overtime for years.

Your exhaustion is real.
Your overwhelm is valid.
Your mental load is heavy — even if no one else sees it.
You deserve rest.
You deserve support.
You deserve to put some of the weight down.
You don't have to hold everything in your mind.
You don't have to be the keeper of all things.
You are allowed to breathe

Reflection

Take a moment to breathe and answer these gently:

1. What are the top five things you mentally keep track of every day?
2. Which of these responsibilities could be shared or delegated?
3. What would it feel like to let go of even one mental task?

A Short Prayer for the Mama carrying the mental load

""Lord, You see the thoughts I carry — the ones I speak and the ones I hold silently. Give me rest from the weight in my mind. Help me release what is too heavy, share what is not mine alone, and trust that I don't have to hold everything together. Guide me toward peace, clarity, and gentleness with myself."

Mama Reminder

Your mind is tired because it has been loving, planning, and protecting everyone.
You deserve a mind that can rest too.

Chapter 9
Coming Home to Yourself: A Compassionate Path to Healing Burnout and Rediscovering Who You Are

You are not lost — you are returning.

There comes a moment in motherhood when you realize you've been running on empty for far too long. Not because you're weak. Not because you're ungrateful. Not because you're doing motherhood wrong.

But because modern motherhood asks you to be everything, everywhere, all at once — without ever stopping to ask: "How are you?"

This chapter is your gentle invitation back to yourself. Back to the woman you were before the exhaustion. Back to the woman you still are beneath the burnout. Back to the woman you are becoming.

The Truth Behind Modern Motherhood

Modern moms are carrying more than any generation before us: The mental load. The emotional labor. The cultural expectations. The guilt. The overstimulation. The pressure to be "strong". The pressure to be "perfect". The pressure to "do it all"

And we do it while…
- *Working*
- *Parenting*
- *Managing homes*
- *Supporting partners*
- *Holding emotions*
- *Holding schedules*
- *Holding everything*

This is not normal.
This is not sustainable.
This is not your fault.

This is the truth behind modern motherhood —and it's why so many mothers feel burned out, lost, and disconnected from themselves.

Burnout Isn't the End — It's a Turning Point

Burnout is not a sign that you're failing. Burnout is a sign that you've been over-functioning in a world that under-supports mothers. Burnout is your body saying: "I need you." Burnout is your heart saying: "Please slow down." Burnout is your soul saying: "Come back to me."

Burnout is not your breaking.
Burnout is your awakening

Somewhere between the school runs, the deadlines, the tantrums, the teenage moods, the meals, the laundry, the mental load, and the emotional labor...

You disappeared.

Not because you wanted to. Not because you weren't paying attention. But because motherhood is loud —and your needs became quiet. You lost:

>Your hobbies
>Your rest
>Your spark
>Your identity
>Your joy
>Your softness
>Your dreams

But here's the truth: You are not gone. You are buried — under exhaustion, expectations, and survival mode. And anything buried can be uncovered again.

Healing Begins With Compassion, Not Perfection

You don't heal burnout by: Working harder, Becoming more organized, Pushing through and Ignoring your needs.

You heal burnout by:

Softening
Slowing
Listening
Resting
Receiving
Reconnecting
Remembering who you are

Healing is not a task. Healing is a homecoming

A Compassionate Path Back to Yourself

Here is the gentle, mother-friendly path to rediscovery:

1. Rest Without Guilt
 Your worth is not measured by productivity.

2. Let Yourself Be Human
 You don't need to be the "strong mom" every day

3. Reconnect With Your Desires
 What do you want?
 What lights you up?
 What makes you feel alive?

4. Rebuild Your Identity Slowly— Not the woman you were before kids —the woman you are becoming now.

5. Allow Support Into Your Life
Healing happens in community, not isolation.

6. Speak Kindly to Yourself
Compassion is the medicine burnout responds to.

Im sure some of you have felt like:
- A shadow of yourself
- A tired version of who you used to be
- A woman who gave everything and kept nothing
- A mother who loved deeply but forgot herself

But healing didn't come from pushing harder. It came from choosing softness. It came from choosing myself — not instead of my children, but alongside them. And you can choose that too.

You are not lost.
You are not broken.
You are not failing.
You are a mother who has been carrying too much,
for too long, with too little support.
And now, it's time to come home to yourself.
You deserve healing.
You deserve rest.
You deserve joy.
You deserve to feel like you again.

Reflection

Take a moment to breathe and answer these gently:

1. What parts of yourself have you forgotten or buried?
2. What does "coming home to myself" mean to you?
3. What is one compassionate step you can take toward healing this week?

A Short Prayer for the Mama returning to herself

"Lord, guide me back to the woman I've forgotten.
Heal the tired parts of me,
restore the hopeful parts of me,
and remind me that I am worthy of rest, joy, and rediscovery.
Help me return to myself with gentleness and grace."

Mama Reminder

You are not meant to disappear inside motherhood.
You are meant to grow inside it.
And you are allowed to find yourself again.

Chapter 10
The Quiet Loneliness Inside a Mother's Heart

You can love your family deeply and still feel alone.

There's a kind of loneliness that mothers carry —a loneliness that doesn't come from being physically alone, but from being emotionally unseen. You can be surrounded by children, partnered, busy, needed, touched, talked to, and still feel like no one truly sees you.

This is the loneliness of modern motherhood —the loneliness that hides behind responsibility, behind routine, behind strength, behind the smile you wear because you don't want to burden anyone. It's the loneliness of being everything for everyone while having no space to be anything for yourself.

Motherhood is full of noise —crying, laughing, calling, asking, needing —but inside that noise is a quiet ache. A longing for:
- Someone to ask how you are
- Someone to notice your exhaustion
- Someone to hold you the way you hold everyone else
- Someone to say "I see you"

- Someone to care for you without you having to ask
- Someone to understand the weight you carry

It's not that you don't love your family. It's that you feel like you've become the background of your own life. And that is a lonely place to be.

Why some Modern Mothers Feel So Alone....

Because you're always giving. Because you're always needed. Because you're always "on." Because you're always the one holding everything together. And because: You don't want to complain, You don't want to seem ungrateful, You don't want to burden anyone, You don't want to admit you're struggling and You don't want to look like you're failing.

So you keep it inside. You keep going. You keep smiling. You keep showing up. And the loneliness grows quietly in the background.

When you're the strong one, the reliable one, the organized one, the emotionally stable one, the one who remembers everything, the one who holds everyone's feelings...People forget that you need support too. They forget that you get tired. They forget that you get overwhelmed. They forget that you need comfort. They forget that you need softness. They forget that you need someone to lean on.

Being the strong one is lonely — because everyone assumes you're okay

And again, I will add my personal experience before, there were days when:
- I was surrounded by people but felt invisible
- I was constantly touched but emotionally untouched
- I was always needed but rarely nurtured
- I was always listening but rarely heard
- I was always giving but rarely receiving

And I would think: Why do I feel so alone when I'm never alone?"

But loneliness isn't about company. It's about connection. It's about being seen. It's about being understood. And mothers often go unseen — not because they're unloved, but because they're so busy loving everyone else....

You Are Not Alone in Feeling Alone

So many mothers feel this way. So many mothers carry this quiet ache. So many mothers wonder if they're the only ones.

You're not. You're part of a generation of women who are:
- Overworked, Overstimulated, Overloaded, Under-supported, Under-rested and Under seen.

Your loneliness is not a personal failure.
It's a symptom of a world that expects mothers to give endlessly without receiving enough in return.

Healing the Loneliness Starts With Being Honest

You don't have to pretend you're fine. You don't have to hide your feelings. You don't have to carry everything alone. Healing begins when you say: "I'm tired." "I'm overwhelmed." "I need help." "I feel lonely." "I need support too." These words are not weakness. They are truth. And truth is where healing begins.

A Gentle Path Out of Loneliness

Here is a compassionate, mother-friendly way to reconnect with yourself and others:

1. Acknowledge your loneliness without shame
Loneliness is not a flaw — it's a signal.

2. Let someone in
A friend, a partner, a sister, a community. You don't have to open everything — just a little.

3. Reconnect with the woman inside the mother
She has needs. She has dreams. She has a voice. She deserves attention too.

4. Create small pockets of connection
A message. A walk. A conversation. A moment of honesty.

5. Allow yourself to receive . . .
Support. Care. Love. Help. You don't have to be the giver all the time.

You are not invisible.
You are not forgotten.
You are not alone.
You are a mother who has been carrying too much,
feeling too much, and holding too much inside.
You deserve connection.
You deserve support.
You deserve to be seen.
You deserve to be held too...

Reflection

Take a moment to breathe and answer these gently:

1. When do you feel the most alone in motherhood?
2. What do you wish someone understood about your daily life?
3. Who is one person you can be more honest with this week?

A Short Prayer for the lonely Mother

"Lord, meet me in the quiet places of my heart.
Fill the spaces where I feel unseen, comfort the parts of me that feel alone,
and surround me with people who understand and support me.
Help me feel connected, valued, and held."

Mama Reminder

You can be surrounded by people and still feel lonely — but you don't have to stay lonely.
You deserve connection, softness, and support too.

Final Chapter
You are coming back to life

This is not the end of your story — it's the beginning of your return.

Mama, take a breath.

You've walked through the heaviness. You've named the exhaustion. You've faced the guilt, the expectations, the loneliness, the burnout, the mental load, the emotional labor, the overstimulation, the truth behind modern motherhood.

And now — here you are.
Still standing.
Still loving.
Still trying.
Still becoming.

This final chapter is not about what you've lost. It's about what you're reclaiming and manifesting.

Motherhood didn't take you away. It stretched you, challenged you, reshaped you, and yes — it tired you. But it did not erase you. You are not a woman who disappeared. You are a woman who is returning....

Returning to her voice.
Returning to her needs.
Returning to her joy.
Returning to her softness.
Returning to her identity.
Returning to her dreams.
Returning to herself.
You are not broken. You are unfolding.

You Are Allowed to Begin or restart Again

You don't need a perfect plan. You don't need a dramatic transformation. You don't need to fix everything at once. You just need one thing: Permission. Permission to rest. Permission to feel. Permission to ask for help. Permission to slow down. Permission to take up space. Permission to rediscover yourself. Permission to choose yourself alongside your children. Permission to begin again — gently, slowly, honestly.

You are allowed to start over at any moment. Even now. Especially now

The Mother You Are Becoming Is Worth Knowing

You are not going back to who you were before motherhood. You are becoming someone wiser, softer, stronger, deeper.

A woman who knows her limits.
A woman who honors her needs.
A woman who listens to her body.
A woman who speaks her truth.
A woman who chooses compassion over guilt.
A woman who is learning to love herself again.
This version of you is worth meeting.
This version of you is worth celebrating.
This version of you is worth becoming

You Are Never Alone on This Journey

Every mother reading this book is walking beside you. Every tired woman, every overwhelmed heart, every quiet soul trying to find her way back — you are part of a sisterhood now. A sisterhood of women who are: healing, rising, rediscovering, reclaiming, rebuilding and remembering who they are

You are not alone. You never were.
You never will be.

You are allowed to rest. You are allowed to heal. You are allowed to grow. You are allowed to change. You are allowed to come back to life. Motherhood is not the end of your story.
It is the beginning of a deeper, more powerful, more compassionate version of you. And you are just getting started

Mama's Final Reminder

You are not done becoming. You are coming back to life — slowly, gently, beautifully. And the world needs the woman you are becoming

Checklist

	Before You Begin
	Find a quiet moment. Place a hand on your heart. Take one slow breath. This is your space — a gentle homecoming....

What Parts of You Are Reawakening?

What parts of yourself have you recently felt flicker back to life?

_____

What moments reminded you that you are still here, still becoming?

_____

What Do You Want to Reclaim?
Think about the woman inside the mother.

- What dreams, hobbies, or desires do you want to reconnect with?
- What parts of your identity feel ready to return?

A Letter to Your Future Self

Write a short letter to the woman you are becoming.

You can begin with:

"I'm proud of you for..." "I hope you remember..." "I want you to feel..."

One Gentle Step Forward

Healing doesn't require big leaps — just one compassionate step. What is one small thing you can do this week to honor yourself?

Acknowledgement

To the mothers who shared their stories, their exhaustion, and their truth — thank you for trusting me with your hearts.

To the women who raised me, shaped me, and showed me what strength looks like — your love is woven into every page.

To my children, who teach me daily about patience, softness, and unconditional love — you are my why.

And to every mama reading this: thank you for letting me walk beside you. Your courage, honesty, and resilience inspired this book

About the Author

Zandra Mae (Zandy) is a Filipina educator, multi-genre author, and mother who writes with honesty, warmth, and cultural depth. As a mentor, guide, a friend you can talk to, , she has spent years supporting women, children , storytellers, and families through compassionate guidance and practical wisdom.

Her work centers on empowering mothers — especially Filipina and migrant women — to navigate burnout, identity loss, and modern motherhood with gentleness and truth.

She lives in Perth, Western Australia, where she creates educational resources, and raises her beautiful family while writing books that speak to the tired, tender hearts of mothers everywhere.

Let's Connect!

Scan Me

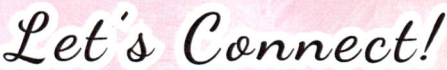

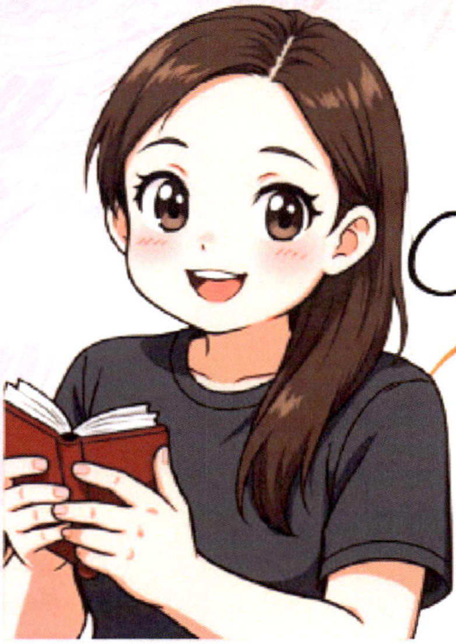

Create with Zandy

COLOURFUL STORIES FOR GROWING HEARTS

@CREATEWITHZANDY

ZANDRAMAECOCHRANEBOOKS.COM

ZANDRAMAECOCHRANE@GMAIL.COM

0432955276

www.ingramcontent.com/pod-product-compliance
Lightning Source LLC
Chambersburg PA
CBRC091503220426
43661CB00020B/1302